DATE DUE	BORROWER'S NAME	ROOM NUMBER
905	Juan	Flores
	OCT 1 5 2015	

THE LIBRARY STORE #43-0802

animal attack!

COYOTE ATTACKS

Suzanne J. Murdico

HIGH interest books

Children's Press
A Division of Grolier Publishing
New York / London / Hong Kong / Sydney
Danbury, Connecticut

For my mother, Barbara Eckert

Photo Credits:p. 4 © FPG/Leonard Lee Rue; p. 7 © Animals Animals/Don Skillman; p. 9 © CORBIS/Paul A. Souders; p. 10 © Animals Animals/E. R. Degginger; p. 13 © CORBIS/Darrell Gulin; p. 15 © CORBIS/James L. Amos; p. 18 © Animals Animals/Joe McDonald; pp. 21, 22, 33 © Animals Animals/ Shane Moore; pp. 22, 25 © FPG/Dennie Cody; p. 26 © CORBIS/Adam Smith Productions; pp. 29, 39 © FPG/Jeri Gleiter; p. 30 © Animals Animals/Gordon and Kathy Illg; p. 35 © Animals Animals/Lynn Stone; pp. 36-37 (spread) © FPG/Telegraph Colour Library

Visit Children's Press on the Internet at:
http://publishing.grolier.com

Library of Congress Cataloging-in-Publication Data

Murdico, Suzanne J.
　　Coyote Attacks / by Suzanne Murdico.
　　　p. cm.—(Animal attack!)
　　Includes bibliographical references (p. 43) and index.
　　Summary: Examines the history of coyote attacks on humans and reasons for
　　　attacks, including loss of habitat. Also looks at coyotes in their natural envi-
　　　ronment and the future existence of coyotes.
　　ISBN 0-516-23313-0 (lib. bdg.)—ISBN 0-516-23513-3 (pbk.)
　　1. Coyotes—Behavior—Juvenile literature. 2. Animal attacks—Juvenile literature.
　　[1. Coyotes.] I. Title.

QL737.C22 M75 2000
599.77′25156 21—dc21
　　　　　　　　　　　　　　　　　　　　　　　　　　99-042405

contents

introduction

In the past, coyotes were found only in forests and other wild areas. However, in recent years coyotes have spread to places where people live. Some coyotes live in the suburbs. Coyotes have even been seen in large cities, such as New York, Los Angeles, and Tucson, Arizona. These coyotes have become more and more aggressive. Sometimes they attack people and pets in their own backyards.

Many years ago, coyotes lived only in the western United States. In the 1800s people began to kill the wolf population. Wolves eat coyotes. With fewer wolves around, the coyote population grew. Coyotes were able to expand their territory. Coyotes are members of the dog family. Today, they can be found throughout North America and Central America.

A coyote howls into the winter air.

chapter one

THE LURE OF LIVESTOCK

Judy Veer runs a farm near Edmonton in Alberta, Canada. One February morning, she went into the field to check on the animals and was greeted by a scary sight. Coyotes had attacked a newborn calf.

"We had our cows calving in a barn, but this one cow had gone off by herself," Veer told a newspaper reporter from the Alberta Report. *"Coyotes had chewed the calf's rectum right out."*

When Veer found the calf, it was still alive but seriously injured. Veer wrapped the baby animal in a blanket. She took the calf to the veterinarian. By that time it was too late to save the calf. The animal had to be put to sleep.

A hungry coyote eats the flesh of a calf it has killed.

COYOTE ATTACKS

Not all coyotes attack livestock, such as cattle and sheep. Yet coyotes are smart animals. They will take advantage of whatever prey (live food) is available. Look at the case of Judy Veer's farm. The winter had been especially mild. Only a small amount of snow had fallen. This meant that a larger than normal number of coyotes had survived the winter. These coyotes needed more food than usual. Veer's newborn calf was just another meal for a hungry coyote.

THE COYOTE AS PREDATOR

Coyotes are omnivorous. This means that they eat both animals and plants. Mostly, coyotes eat small rodents, such as mice, squirrels, and rabbits. Yet coyotes are not picky eaters. They will eat just about any food that they can find. Coyotes will eat insects, fruit, berries, and carrion. Carrion is the rotting flesh of animals that died or were killed by other animals.

Coyotes may also eat domestic animals. Domestic animals include cats, small dogs, and

A sheep's head is all that is left after the animal was attacked and eaten by coyotes.

livestock. In fact, some experts say that coyotes kill more sheep and cattle than all other predators combined. The coyotes most likely to attack livestock are those with hungry pups (baby coyotes) to feed.

Finding Food

Coyotes usually hunt for food at night. They run at speeds up to 25 to 30 miles per hour (40 to 48 kph). Coyotes can sprint at 40 miles per hour (64 kph). A coyote may travel more than one hundred miles each night in search of food.

With their sharp senses of sight and hearing, coyotes are able to locate even the smallest prey. Their vision is so good that they can spot the tiniest movement across a field. Their sense of hearing is so fine that they can detect mice moving around beneath the snow.

Coyotes are highly adaptable. This means they can survive in many different environments. One reason for this is that they can change their diet to suit the place in which they live. Coyotes will simply find whatever prey or other food is available. They will even eat garbage left by humans!

ATTACK STRATEGY

Coyotes plan their attacks on animals. If the animal

A coyote howls under a full moon.

is large, such as a deer, the coyote will lunge for the animal's throat. The coyote's jaws lock down and choke the animal to death.

If the prey is small, such as a squirrel, the coyote will use its jaws to crush it to death. The coyote may even carry off the small animal while it's still alive. Sometimes a coyote will find an animal that is help-less. This animal might be injured or newly born. In this case, the coyote may simply eat it alive.

Coyotes are very determined hunters. Professor Rex O. Baker is a leading expert on coyote attacks. He told *Outdoor Life* magazine that this behavior is part of a coyote's being a wild animal. Baker said that coyotes have different ways of doing things, like hunting or attacking. These are called modes. "When coyotes are in 'attack mode,' they stay focused on their prey. They may even return time and time again, just looking for a chance to kill."

Tricks of the Trade

Coyotes often hunt alone. However, they may also

A coyote carries a goose in its jaws.

work together to kill large domestic animals. Sometimes sheep or cattle are being guarded by dogs. Coyotes usually work in pairs to attack the livestock. Recently, though, coyotes have found a better way to outsmart the guard dogs. The coyotes have started to work in packs of four to eight. One or two coyotes act as decoys to distract the dogs. Then the other coyotes will kill a sheep or cow.

The clever coyotes have another trick up their sleeves. Although they normally hunt at night, they will sometimes attack the livestock during the day. This way, the coyotes are attacking when the guard dogs are tired after having stayed up all night protecting the herd.

Working Together

Coyotes also work in packs during the winter to kill larger prey, such as deer and elk. Sometimes they work together as a sort of relay team. One coyote will chase the animal in a circle. When that coyote begins to tire, another coyote takes up the chase. Now the first coyote can rest. By taking turns, the coyotes stay fresh while the hunted animal becomes worn out. After a while the animal will lose its battle with the coyotes.

Coyotes often work in groups to capture prey, like these three that have killed an elk.

Coyotes even work with other types of animals to hunt. If a badger is digging at the burrow of an animal living underground, a coyote will wait for its chance to steal the prey. Sometimes the underground animal may try to escape from the badger by leaving from a different hole. If it does, the coyote will chase it down. However, if the animal stays in the hole, the badger will get its meal.

SURVIVAL STRATEGIES

The large coyote population causes problems for ranchers. These ranchers have livestock that may be attacked and killed by coyotes. Ranchers have begun hunting coyotes. They also trap and poison many coyotes. However, this plan to kill off the coyote population has failed.

When the coyote population is threatened, the coyotes have a special way of surviving. Coyotes will begin having babies earlier. Instead of having pups at two years old they

did you know?

Desert coyotes weigh only 20 pounds (9 kg). This is half as much as mountain coyotes. Also, desert coyotes have shorter, thinner fur so their bodies can release more heat to help them stay cool.

will have them at one year old. Also, the coyotes will begin to have more pups. They'll have six to eight pups per litter instead of the normal three to four. In this way, coyotes are able to maintain their population.

In the past one hundred years, 20 million coyotes have been killed. Yet the number of coyotes today is higher than it has ever been. Humans have tried to kill coyotes for many reasons. However, the coyote population is alive and well. Each generation of coyotes passes down its knowledge of survival to the next generation. This makes future generations of coyotes even smarter and more able to protect themselves from harm.

chapter two

ATTACKS ON PEOPLE

Three-year-old Daniel Neal was playing on a swing set in the backyard of his home on Cape Cod, Massachusetts. Suddenly, a coyote appeared in the yard. The animal jumped on the child. The coyote began scratching and biting Daniel on his head, shoulders, and back.

The boy's mother heard screaming and ran outside to find the coyote attacking her son. She fought with the animal. She hit it on the head with her hands. Finally she was able to pull the coyote off her child. Even then, the coyote would not go away. The animal was determined to kill the young boy. The coyote was still hiding in the yard when the

A coyote overlooks a suburban home.

police arrived. A police officer shot and killed the animal. Daniel was taken to the hospital, but his injuries were not serious.

WHY COYOTES ATTACK PEOPLE

This attack on Cape Cod happened in 1998. It was the first coyote attack on a human in the state of Massachusetts. Although coyote attacks on humans are unusual, they have been occurring more often in recent years. Between 1988 and 1998, more than fifty people in California were attacked by coyotes. There are two main reasons for the increase in coyote attacks. One is the loss of open land where coyotes can live. The other reason is that coyotes have lost their fear of humans.

Loss of Habitat

Coyotes live in the wild. This is their home, called their habitat. As human populations grow, more wild lands disappear. More homes, offices, and shopping centers are built. The coyotes who once

Houses are often built where coyotes have lived. Now many coyotes live closer to humans.

lived in these areas must now look for new places to live. They must hunt for food in different places as well. As their habitat shrinks, coyotes move closer to areas where people live.

"Coyotes normally avoid people, but as both human and wildlife populations continue to grow, the chance for attacks increases," Carter Luke told the *Environmental News Network*. Luke is vice

COYOTE ATTACKS

At first glance, coyotes look like dogs. Beware! These are wild animals.

president for Humane Services at the Massachusetts Society for the Prevention of Cruelty to Animals.

Loss of Fear

Coyotes are part of the dog family. Their Latin name is *canis latrans,* which means "barking dog." They look very similar to the German shepherd breed of dog, only smaller in size. The main difference between coyotes and dogs is that coyotes have a bushy tail that hangs down below the level of the back. Dogs carry their tails curved upward. Coyotes also have a narrower snout than dogs. An adult coyote is between 30 and 50 inches long (76–127cm). Coyotes weigh between 25 and 40 pounds (11–18kg).

Because coyotes look so similar to dogs, some people treat them as dogs. People may feed the coyotes. Sometimes they throw coyotes scraps of food. Other times they may leave pet food outside or leftovers in open trash cans. The coyotes can find and eat the food. This is how coyotes become used to seeing people and being around people. For this reason, they often lose their natural fear of humans. Coyotes then start to link humans with food. This is when coyotes sometimes begin to view humans as food.

URBAN COYOTES

When coyotes lose their natural habitat, they easily adapt to a new environment. This happened in the desert city of Tucson, Arizona. When desert lands were cleared and developed for use by humans, coyotes simply moved into the city. The coyotes continued to eat their usual rodent prey. However, the number of attacks on people has risen. This is because these urban coyotes have learned to expect food from people. The coyotes have become aggressive when they haven't gotten a handout. Sometimes a small child looks like food to a hungry coyote.

Coyotes have also moved into cities in the eastern United States, including New York City. In the

Coyotes are now used to being around humans. Sometimes you can see a coyote walking down a suburban street.

Bronx, one of the city's five boroughs, coyotes have been spotted hiding in a cemetery. A pair of coyotes were also found living in New York City's famous Central Park.

Urban coyotes (and suburban ones too) can find plenty of sources of food and water. Besides

Coyotes living near towns and cities must cross streets and highways. This is dangerous for both motorists and the animals.

their usual prey, they eat food from trash cans and garbage dumps, and pet food left outside. Coyotes even eat people's pets. Water is easy to find for coyotes. They drink from birdbaths, lawn sprinklers, and public fountains. The biggest problem for coyotes living in the city is the automobile. Just like other animals, coyotes are sometimes the victims of traffic accidents.

SUBURBAN COYOTES

More and more coyotes have been seen walking

the streets of suburban towns. In 1997, four-year-old Lauren Bridges was playing in the snow in South Lake Tahoe, California, when she was attacked by a coyote. The coyote bit Lauren's head and hands before her father was able to pull the animal away from the little girl. Lauren received several cuts and wounds from bites. Luckily, her wounds were not serious. She was treated and released from the hospital. A police officer shot and killed the coyote that had attacked her.

Dan Hinz, a wildlife biologist with the Department of Fish and Game, explained that this type of attack is unusual. "It's just very rare for a coyote to attack a person," he told a news reporter from the *Mountain Democrat*. "They see people and they usually head the other way." However, coyote attacks on small children are happening more often.

Attacks on Children

Another attack on a child took place in 1997 in Fullerton, California. This town is just a few miles from Disneyland. Three-year-old Jennifer Dimmick was playing in a sandbox with several other children. A coyote had been watching the children from some bushes just a few feet away. As Jennifer started walking home, the coyote leaped out of the bushes and knocked down the little girl.

The coyote lunged for Jennifer's neck. Jennifer fought back. She punched and kicked the animal. The coyote began biting the child's chest and legs. Jennifer's mother heard her daughter's screams. She came out of their house and ran across the street to help. She found her daughter scared and bloody but alive. Just a few days after the attack, Jennifer and her father walked through their neighborhood and passed out flyers to warn people about coyotes.

Newport Beach, California, is a suburb near Los Angeles. One day a two-year-old boy got too close to a coyote. The boy's father noticed the coyote watching his son in the backyard of their home. The father quickly grabbed the boy before the coyote had a chance to attack. The coyote

A coyote rests in a meadow.

returned to the backyard at the same time for four days in a row. Finally, the coyote was trapped and taken away from the area.

chapter three

PETS AS PREY

The Akers family lives on a military base in Alaska. They own a small brown-and-white Pekinese puppy named Rocky. One day, a neighbor named Pat was looking out his second-floor window. Pat noticed something small and brown on a snowy field outside. Using a pair of binoculars, he could see that the brown spot was actually Rocky. Not far from Rocky was a coyote eating the body of a dead moose. A second coyote lay hidden back toward the woods. Pat went outside to rescue Rocky. He was a little late. Before he could reach the dog, one of the coyotes bit the little dog on the head and neck. Rocky was still alive,

Sharp teeth and a snarling face spell danger.

though. Pat picked up the wounded dog and carried him inside.

"Rocky was probably just a snack," Pat told a reporter from the *Anchorage Daily News.* "I expect the coyote was going to finish him off after lunch."

Rocky was lucky. Although he was injured, he survived this coyote attack. Many cats and dogs who cross paths with coyotes are not so lucky.

THE CRAFTY COYOTE

Have you ever wondered where the cartoon character Wile E. Coyote got his name? Coyotes are extremely wily, or sly. They may watch the owner of a cat or dog. Coyotes can figure out the person's daily habits and schedule. They will wait until the pet owner is away from home. Then they come back and attack the pet.

"Coyotes see pets as food," Erik Amati, a Massachusetts game biologist, explained to an

A coyote's back hunches and its ears stand up when it hunts for food.

Associated Press reporter. "In a lot of cases we've seen cats being taken and dogs being attacked and killed."

DISAPPEARING PETS

Coyotes in Marshfield, Massachusetts, have attacked some pets and caused others to disappear. During one recent summer, a coyote killed and ate part of a cocker spaniel. Norma Haskins, an animal control officer in Marshfield, reported that many cats had mysteriously disappeared, as well.

"We've also had about sixty cats missing over the summer. That's almost twice our normal number," Haskins told the *Associated Press*. "We have a feeling the coyotes are eating some of them."

In suburban Westminster, Colorado, coyotes are often seen walking through people's back-yards. In a single month, coyotes killed at least eleven dogs and many more cats. People began keeping their pets indoors.

Coyotes must be fast to hunt and survive in the wild.

THE COYOTES' FUTURE

In Native American culture, the coyote is known as "The Trickster." In some Native American languages, the coyote is called the "Song Dog" because of its noticeable "songs," or howls. These sounds are used to alert other members of the pack to the coyote's location.

A lone desert coyote "singing" in the American Southwest.

Native Americans have great respect for coyotes. They understand that the coyotes' cleverness and natural instincts will help the species to survive. There is a Native American legend about the future of coyotes: When humans and other living creatures are gone from the Earth, only the coyote will remain.

Helpful or Harmful?

Coyotes may always be one of nature's most misunderstood animals. Many farmers and ranchers consider them pests that kill their livestock. However, coyotes also help farmers by killing the field mice, rats, and other rodents. These rodents eat farm crops. Many experts believe coyotes are a helpful and important part of the food chain. Without coyotes, rodent populations and other unwanted pests would grow quickly and cause many problems.

Living with Coyotes

Humans continue to build on lands once used by coyotes. This means that coyotes will continue to move into populated areas. Even though coyotes and people live close together, there are few attacks on humans. Each year, more dogs than coyotes bite people. However, people need to change their behavior toward coyotes. That way they can avoid being attacked by coyotes.

People must keep in mind that coyotes are wild animals. If people don't feed coyotes and treat them like pets, coyotes will keep their natural fear of humans. Coyotes will then stay away from humans. This fear will then be passed down, and future generations of coyotes will learn to avoid humans.

A mountain coyote

FACT SHEET

Species
Coyote (*canis latrans*)

Geographic Location

North America—including western and southern
   Canada, the continental United States, and
   Mexico. Also, parts of Central America.

Life Span

Three to four years

The coyote heads on the map show
where coyotes are found in North
America and parts of Central America

new words

adaptable able to adjust for survival

burrow a hole in the ground made by an animal and used for shelter

carrion rotting flesh of a dead animal

domestic animal an animal that is tame and kept as a pet

environment the things, people, and places that surround you

habitat an area where an animal naturally lives and grows

livestock farm animals, such as cattle and sheep, that are raised for food or profit

nocturnal being active at night

omnivorous eating both animal and plant matter

opportunistic taking advantage of whatever is available for survival

predator an animal that hunts and kills other animals

prey an animal that is killed and eaten for food

territory an area that is occupied and defended by an animal or group of animals

veterinarian a doctor who treats injuries and diseases in animals

for further reading

Grady, Wayne. *The World of the Coyote.* San Francisco: Sierra Club Books, 1994.

Hodge, Deborah. *Wild Dogs: Wolves, Coyotes and Foxes.* Toronto: Kids Can Press Ltd., 1997.

Lepthien, Emilie U. *Coyotes.* Chicago: Childrens Press, 1993.

Samuelson, Mary Lou, and Gloria G. Schlaepfer. *The Coyote.* New York: Dillon Press, 1993.

Swan, Erin Pembrey. *Land Predators of North America.* Danbury, CT: Franklin Watts, 1999.

Winner, Cherie, *Coyotes.* Minneapolis: Carolrhoda Books, Inc., 1995.

resources

Organizations
Endangered Wildlife Trust
346 Smith Ridge Road
New Canaan, CT 06840
(203) 966-2748
Web site: www.ewt.org

Sierra Club
85 Second Street, 2nd Floor
San Francisco, CA 94105-3441
(415) 977-5500
Web site: www.sierraclub.org

Web Sites
Animal Attack Files
http://www.igorilla.com/gorilla/animal/
This site offers a great selection of news articles describing recent attacks on humans by animals.

Included is a link to book lists for further reading.

COYOTE Magazine
http://www.expage.com/page/mrsganimalcoyote
Here's a place to learn more about coyotes and what they look like, their daily routine, and their hunting and eating habits. This site also includes some great pictures of coyotes!

DesertUSA Magazine
http://www.desertusa.com/
This is a great site to learn about deserts and all those plants and animals to be found in a desert, including coyotes. They aren't just filled with sand and cactuses!

National Wildlife Federation
http://www.nwf.org/

The NWF deals with all wild animals. It's a good site to find out about teen adventure programs, read articles on wildlife, and learn how the NWF works toward animal conservation.

index

About the Author

Suzanne J. Murdico is a freelance writer who specializes in educational books. She has a degree in English and is the author of ten nonfiction books for children and teens. Suzanne has always loved animals. She did her college internship in the public relations department at the Philadelphia Zoo. Suzanne lives in New Jersey with her husband and their two tabby cats.